A phenomenon that has the scale of the universe and affects all aspects of our life in an understandable and easy form is depicted for children's perception and the development of interest in space. A planetary parade is an astronomical phenomenon where several planets line up in a single line relative to the sun.

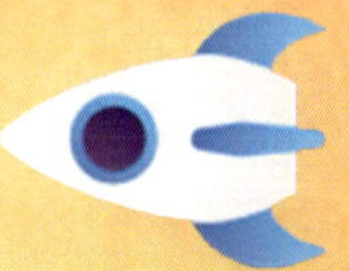

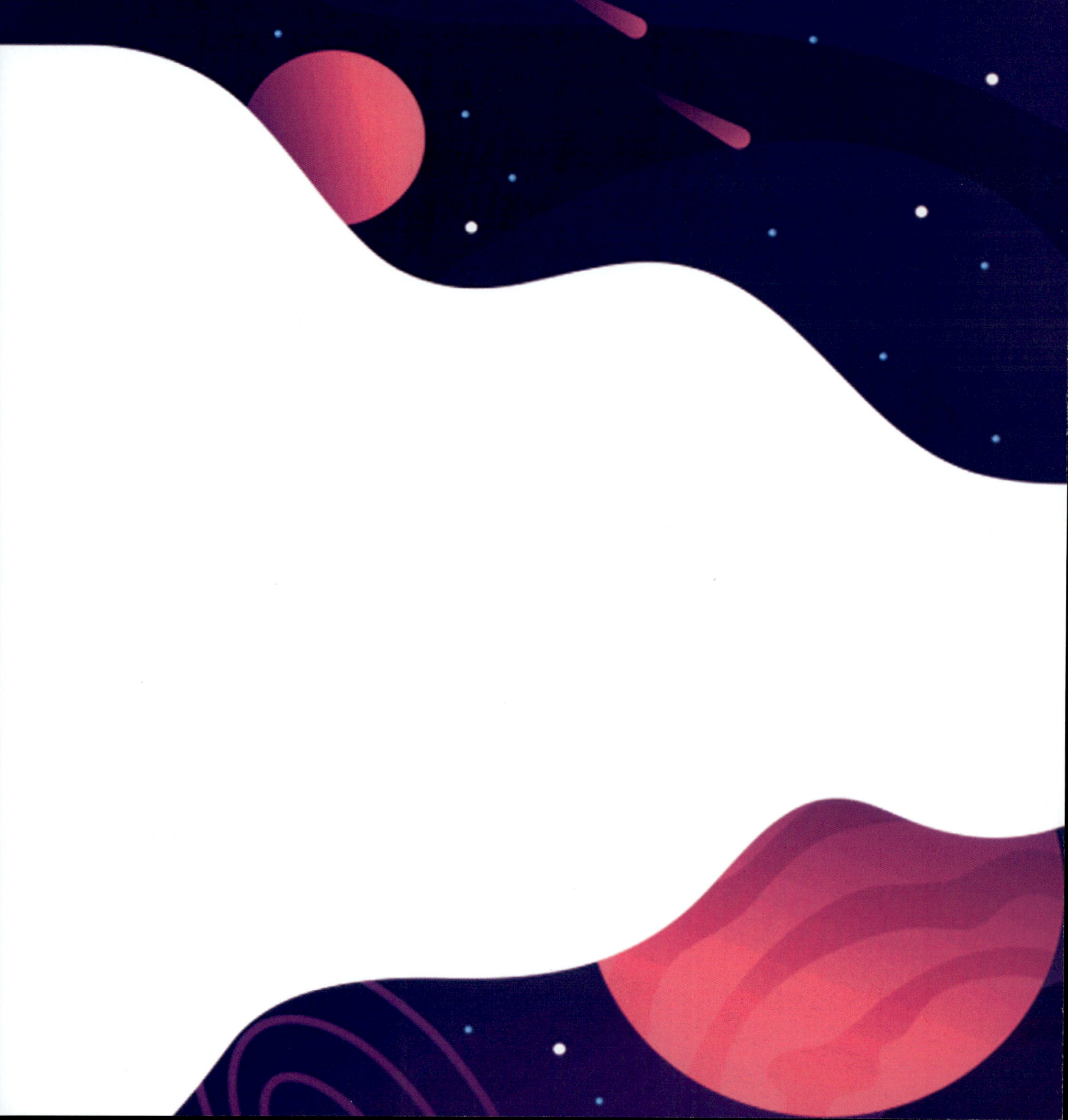

PARADE of PLANETS

Artem H.

AUSTIN MACAULEY PUBLISHERS™
LONDON • CAMBRIDGE • NEW YORK • SHARJAH

ISBN – 9789948803096 - (Paperback)
ISBN – 9789948803102 - (E-Book)

Application Number: MC-10-01-2891947
Age Classification: E

Printer Name: iPrint Global Ltd
Printer Address: Witchford, England

First Published 2023
AUSTIN MACAULEY PUBLISHERS FZE
Sharjah Publishing City
P.O Box [519201]
Sharjah, UAE
www.austinmacauley.ae
+971 655 95 202

Planet Earth decided to prepare and check the readiness of other planets for the upcoming parade of planets.

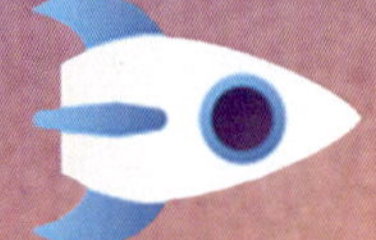

At the first the Earth turned
to her close friend, the Moon,
but she asked to wait a little
as she was now busy with a
solar eclipse.

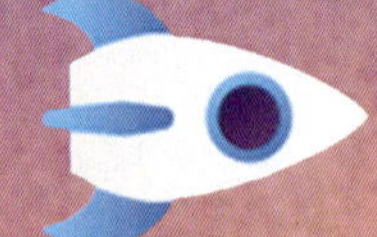

Then the Earth began to ask Venus and Mercury about the upcoming parade. Although these planets were closest to the Sun, they knew what was happening in other parts of the galaxy.

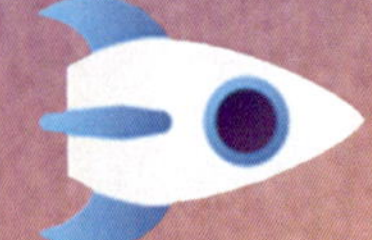

After a solar eclipse, the
Moon reminded the Earth
that she would tell about the
parade to Mars.

Mars understood that in order to further inform the news of the parade to other planets, it was necessary to go through a difficult part.

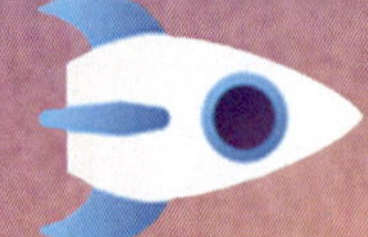

A whole asteroid belt.

Saturn, having learned
about the parade of planets,
decided to immediately tell
Jupiter, the largest planet in
our solar system, about it.

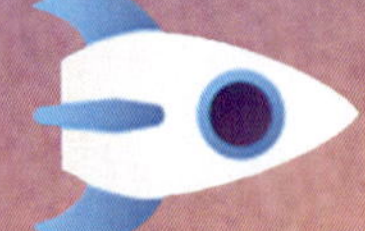

His majesty is Jupiter.

Three planets very far from the Earth – Saturn, Pluto and Uranus – were the last to know about the parade.

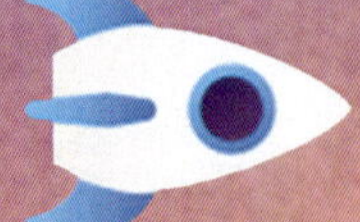

Let's check our watches as time goes on differently on every planet.

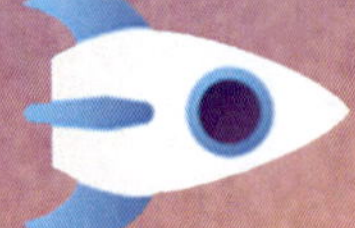

We are ready.

Parade of planets.

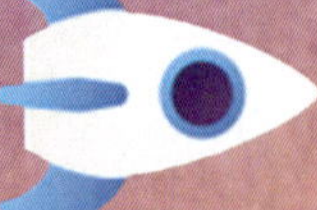

Yes! We did it. The next parade will only be in many, many years.

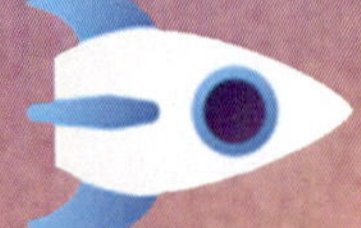

Thank you for your interest in this topic, look at the stars more often and maybe you can find answers to the many riddles of the Universe.